"𝒥nner 𝒲hispers"

Messages From A Spirit Guide

Volume II

April Crawford

"Inner Whispers": Messages From A Spirit Guide
(Volume II)

Author: April Crawford

Publisher: Connecting Wave
2629 Foothill Blvd.
Unit # 353
La Crescenta, CA 91214
www.ConnectingWave.com

ISBN: 978-0-9823269-5-4

For Author Information: www.AprilCrawford.com

Other books via April Crawford:
www.AprilCrawfordBookStore.com

Book Design: Allen Crawford

For Permissions: Publisher@ConnectingWave.com

CONTENTS

CONTENTS

CONTENTS

CONTENTS

***

Forward by **VERONICA**

Many writings have been shared during the path of "Inner Whispers". All of them... through the gracious hand of April who allows us, VERONICA, to speak.

Our intention is to reach out to those who feel sharply, the isolation of physical. Spirit is more accustomed to the blend, which most of you seek throughout your incarnation.

We understand the process.

Never feel alone for we are always focused on the souls of those who need assistance. It is our intention to enlighten and to share a perspective to help you on your journey home. We have great affection for your soul.

The longevity of our relationship supersedes the writing of this book.

Forward by VERONICA

Though without physical form, we are not without heart & compassion for those evolving their way through the physical experience. 'Tis the reason for our participation... no other.

Feel our presence and be comforted. We are indeed real, our consciousness ever expanding towards evolution. Our hope is that you will journey with us to the eternal. We are merely participating at a different frequency and sometimes it provides a clearer view.

We are your constant supporter with true belief in the power of your soul.

Your friend,

VERONICA

About April Crawford

April Crawford is a natural Open Deep Trance Channel and Spirit Medium. These are relatively rare.

Because April is able to be completely open and without any fear of the process whatsoever, the nonphysical entities and guides who come through are able to <u>totally</u> integrate with the physical, while at the same time not blending at all with April's personality. They therefore have <u>full</u> physical and emotional, control during their "visits".

This allows zero distortion or "coloring" by April, and also allows them to walk around the room, go out for a walk in the night air, keep their eyes wide open when they speak, and even eat or drink if they wish (but most choose not to).

These physical abilities are one of the things that allow VERONICA... the name we have given to the highly evolved nonphysical entity and guide that gave us most of the messages in this book... to give readings and have long fully interactive conversations over a speakerphone, and even to write in longhand herself (not automatic writing), or type on a computer keyboard and even use a computer mouse or computer touch screen.

You can see videos of VERONICA speaking while April Crawford is in deep trance at:

www.AprilCrawford.com

April routinely allows many different entities and aspects of entities to come through, and they have a full range of motion and emotion. Some who are in-between physical lives, for example, have cried uncontrollably or expressed total joy when we advised them of certain things about their physical lives.

About VERONICA

The Spirit Guide that wrote all of these messages is VERONICA. There are a few others that have added some quotes for the day also, and they are noted.

"VERONICA", as we call "her", is an evolved nonphysical entity and guide. "She" refers to herself as a nonphysical consciousness and she leans toward female energy even though VERONICA has been both sexes and she has told me her favorite physical life was as a male.

(Note: Some other entities and individuals in-between physical lives that come through April Crawford express

About VERONICA

themselves as male energies, so it is not because April is female that VERONICA expresses herself as female.)

You may wonder about VERONICA's name. Actually, it is a name we gave her many years ago. When she first came through, it was rather amazing and rather dramatic (and VERONIA was not the first to come through, but was certainly the most intense). At that time, "she" did not give us a name when we asked, saying basically that "Labels are not necessary". She went on to say that if we needed a label, that we could choose whatever name we wanted.

We chose the name "VERONICA", and it stuck. Now, even other nonphysical beings who visit via April Crawford's Open Deep Trance Channeling know exactly who VERONICA is. It seems that things get around in the cosmos rather quickly and rather completely!

All of VERONICA's messages are either spoken or written by her in first, final, and only draft. There is never any editing of a single sentence or word.

53

<u>The Current State of Affairs</u>

"We are often asked to comment on the current state of affairs in your cultures worldwide. It appears from your viewpoint that all is collapsing into a downward spiral that will end in the destruction of the reality that all of you currently reside in.

The sphere that provides all with an environment of choice is a living energy as well as you are. It responds to the energy it feels while breathing within an internal pulse. All is energy.

It ebbs and flows with an electrical current that is biological in nature... as you are. This movement has pulsated for many of your current calendar years if one were to calculate it by that standard.

From our own perspective this sphere has had great movement for over millions of your years. Civilizations too many to record have participated upon this place and others.

By no means is this the only location of creation. There are many energy vortexes.

Since we are outside the timeline all is available, your past, present and probable futures.

Groupings of souls have incarnated in many civilizations that have risen and fallen. Some of you recall them, others do not. However, that does not dictate the reality.

We would say that the underlying negativity attached to all of the perceived downward spirals, no matter what timeline, has been the lack of respect. This includes the planet, towards each other and to the cores of your own souls.

So we say that if indeed you wish to divert this perceived negative spiral begin by looking at your life. Respect all energy no matter how different it may appear to you. This environment was created by a diverse group of entities. Each with unique perspectives.

Respect each other. Respect nature. The linear list is infinite.

Incorporate respect in your lives. Each of you is a unique manifestation. It was not intended for all to be a homogenized manifestation. The uniqueness was intentional perhaps so respect would be learned.

One may disagree with anything, but respect for it should never be an option."

-VERONICA

"You see, I am what you would term dead. I can still communicate, however, certainly a surprise to me."

From: Rachel in "Parting Notes":
A Connection with the Afterlife

54

Clutter in The Linear

"Participating in life with the best intent and desire can still leave one feeling despondent over the lack of progress. "Life" surely appears to get in the way of spiritual awareness. Some religious movements prescribe the leaving of linear pursuits to embrace only spiritual. Others embrace a focusing of thought while still others teach a symbolic regimen of ritual to clear one's path to heaven.

With all the methods available why are there still so many seemingly lost in a clutter of drama that gives no meaning to their lives?

From our perspective the soul's intention should be the most predominant voice in the hearts of all. However, that can be difficult with all the clutter accumulated in one's life.

Despair arises in the soul when its true voice cannot be heard.

Linear has accelerated in your current cultures. There is no longer the silence of a winter day where one can almost hear snow falling. Technology has replaced the pulse of the heart leaving some species needing to vacate the linear altogether.

We have heard from many of you who are worried about the environment created from the calm whispers of our souls... its core fiber frayed from creations that come energy tense with clutter of the linear.

It is important to think quietly while setting aside the trivia of your day. Participate in your own personal meditation while creating the intention of your soul. It's not lost, nor is your environment. It's merely out of touch, misplaced in the dramatic events of your day.

Spiritual progress can be achieved easily with clearer thought. How long has it been since you experienced an eternal moment? If you cannot recall then we beseech your focus upon that from which you came..... your entity.

Quiet. Slower pace. Clear thought. Eliminate that which is not necessary. You do not have to depend upon your external to provide the moment. It is you that creates all. If everyone made that a priority your linear would become less cluttered allowing the magnificence of your soul to shine through.

All would align... including your environment."

-VERONICA

"Nothing is gained from negativity."

From: VERONICA

55

<u>Appreciation</u>

"While one participates in the linear it is important to value what has been given from your eternal energy. Your life may be filled with drama but the intention of the soul is ever present. Your thoughts create the choices and the choices made determine how the linear is played out.

There is great confusion when more focus is given to the linear than the eternal energy. Definition of connection is often lost in what some perceive as a difficult incarnation. There can be a feeling of despair as one moves more into the drama instead of pausing to appreciate their soul.

Of course there are many schools of thought on the subject. Whilst honoring all of them, we merely wish to point out the core energy needed to create one's reality. It is extremely important to understand and appreciate the soul's ability.

The soul being ever hopeful & energetic wishes to eliminate negativity and drama. If there is a separation the thought process can create negative moments. Thought is the tool to change and create your reality. Its connection with the soul energy is the key to opening a connection between them.

No matter what negative circumstances you find yourself in, a reversal is available through an appreciation of your soul energy.

How does one do that?

We would say forgiveness of the self for past negative choices and to seek a reconnection to the self. Instead of cursing one's life perhaps a simple moment of gratitude for the life would be appropriate.

Nothing is gained from negativity. Seek the one good moment in your life. No matter what you feel there is always one good moment. Attach to the feeling of that energy & recreate the moment. Align with your soul. If given the opportunity it will redeem a negative perspective.

Appreciate the life your soul has created. It is special and unique. If you are unhappy a return to the soul is necessary."

-VERONICA

**"If you haven't guessed, I'll give you a clue,
the master of the universe is inside of you..."**

From: The Reflections of a Spiritual Astronaut Books

56

Belief Systems

"When a soul incarnates into the linear it often decides upon a belief system to provide itself with a contact with the soul. Depending upon the soul level the belief system may help propel the energy into more profound evolvement.

We honor all belief systems, however, there may be times where the system should be altered to keep up with the soul. This is not a simple moment for most but an actual evolution that can occur within the linear.

In most cases the belief system is built upon a cultural moment. Therefore, the larger picture is not as clear as it would be from an eternal soul perspective. Linear circumstance provides a merging that is not easy to disengage from when one seeks to evolve.

We are not diminishing the relevance of belief systems. The relevance is determined by the singular energy involved. We only wish to point out that belief systems are linear, an attempt to define the eternal from a linear point of view. The soul wishes to manifest fully while the linear viewpoint may be hindered by a strict belief that really is not relevant in the full perspective of the soul.

So we advise that all who wish to evolve should respect all belief systems and become more attached to the soul in general. Belief systems may come and go in the manifestations provided by the soul. What is important is that the soul continues the progress un-hindered by the linear perspectives.

The linear is a tool to evolve, not a statement of the soul.

Belief systems are a product of the linear in its attempt to understand the eternal. Sometimes accurate... and sometimes not."

-VERONICA

"Your present is the grand opportunity.
Energize it."

From: VERONICA

57

<u>Letting Go of the Past</u>

"In your lifetime many choices are made that result in a negative outcome. The desire of the soul to evolve participates fully seeking all experience. The linear self engages in the negativity often magnifying the energy beyond what it needs to be.

We speak to many who are involved in a repetitive negative linear seeking resolution from their choices.

It is first most important to release past choices consciously. Whatever they were they have brought you to this moment of clarity.

Your emotions play a huge part of this cycle so self forgiveness is also an imperative part of the process.

See clearly the reason behind the past moments and the value of release. This clearing of energy will allow your creative process to continue in a more positive way.

The past cannot be erased. It is a part of your experience, however, by releasing the energy behind it through forgiveness will help your energy to regain its integrity. Connect to your source energy and forgive. It is the first step to creating a more beneficial future.

Your present is the grand opportunity.

Energize it."

-VERONICA

58

<u>Evolvement Through Difficult Situations</u>

"When one decides to participate in the linear the eternal perspective available offers comfort of the end result. Upon manifesting in the time-line the physical consciousness tends to disassociate with the larger viewpoint.

The condensed perspective is intense, often leading the individual into despair.

Difficult situations are sometimes necessary for the soul to evolve, and are created purposefully by the individual.

We realize the unpopularity of such a creative moment when one is considering the probabilities, however, it is true that some lessons require a strong experience for evolution to occur.

The evolved perspective considers the experience and often in hindsight knows that even the most negative experience can produce a positive outcome.

The trick is to survive the moment to reap the benefits of the experience. Support from eternal energy is available, but not always called upon in the appropriate manner.

Remember that you are an eternal energy having a physical experience, not the other way around.

Instead of bemoaning the creation contemplate the information received and move forward.

Stay true to your soul and its energy, and receive the lessons and use them to move forward. Often while physical the recreation of the events occur until one comes to that conclusion.

Learn the lesson and move forward. Forgive but do not forget the moment. Difficulty can be replaced by easiness if one pays close enough attention.

Again, we realize the reluctance of those stuck in a negative pattern to receive this information, however, we feel the infinitive power of the Soul and align our energies with it, so as to help you through it.

You are not alone."

-VERONICA

"The Light, where doubt does not exist,

easily encompasses anything..."

From: The Reflections of a Spiritual Astronaut Books

'

59

<u>Connecting with Spirit Guides</u>

"Wherever you are in the timeline of linear, the idea of spiritual guides most likely has crossed your mind.

Who are they?

What are they?

Is an introduction possible?

What are their names?

These questions have filled most of you with a never ending quest to connect with them in some way. Every "incarnated" soul has around them energies who assist with aligning internal energy. Some have been with you since birth, some move in and out according to the issues at hand. Some have never been physical while others may have had a relationship with you in a previous linear.

As varied of an experience that it may be, the one underlying true moment is their commitment to you.

No matter what choices you make they are ever at your side to assist energetically. They cannot make decisions for your but can attempt to align your energy appropriately.

However you may define yourself, be assured that your guides see the whole picture and make no judgments.

The spirit guide's presence is unconditional and persistent. In other words..... they do not give up on you.... ever.

This everlasting support is available for the entire life regardless if you are aware of it or not. The key is to become aware so as to find support while moving through your life."

-VERONICA

"We write...for the reassurance to you that there is more. It is not like anything you could imagine right now. You will remember when you open your spiritual eyes. There will be rejoicing. Do not fear death. That is our message to you."

From: T Mary in "Parting Notes":
A Connection with the Afterlife.

60

<u>Spirit Guides II</u>

"Spirit guides are pure energy vibrating in a compatible way with your own. In the incarnation process the linear energy can become out of sync making it difficult for smooth communication. Most would prefer the dialogue to be conversational but in desperation would settle for a word.

To become more aligned, the linear soul (you) should attempt separating from the daily chitter chatter that accumulates in one's mind. This can be achieved in many ways and we suggest that the standard process of meditation may not be appropriate for all.

Seek calmness in a way suitable for your own energy. One can spend much linear time participating in a meditation process that is not aligned with them.

It is also important to understand that outside of the timeline energy does not participate in verbal language or events. The vibration resonates more predominantly non-linearly. So there is probability that communication will be more energetic at times manifesting as a feeling or inclination.

This is not to say that verbal communication does not exist. It is stated to remind you that linear is not the only path and to not be disappointed if words are not readily available.

The same holds true for names and labels. Energies often have participated in many experiences, thus referring to themselves as "us" rather than "I". Outside of the linear the multiplicity of participation makes a single name or label irrelevant.

We realize though the importance of such labels to those participating in a "life". The guide may indulge and take a familiar name they have incarnated as. Or they may simply agree to a label that has meaning for you.

It's not the name that is so important as the energy flow of the relationship."

-VERONICA

**"The way to abundance does not begin externally.
It begins in that place of wonder called your soul..."**

From: The Reflections of a Spiritual Astronaut Books

61

Spirit Guides III
Maintaining a relationship with
Spirit Guides

"Linear participation is a great opportunity for condensed experience for the soul. It was intended for all to feel the individuality of the moments while staying connected to the vastness of spiritual.

The soul may have difficulties adjusting to the singleness and perceived separation because of the intensity of the energy required to incarnate. One may feel great spiritual loneliness and not be able to define the roots of it.

Soul energy has a connected memory of oneness that sustains most though the physical journey. The feeling of separation is born when situations and dramas become out of control for various reasons. When the soul perceives itself without the support of the non-linear it will often engage in a variety of negativity including depression, anger, disappointment and disillusionment.

The spirit guide gives the soul an opportunity to reconnect in a "linear way" while re-igniting the energy needed to engage whatever the intended purpose might be.

Therefore, the relationship between yourself and your guides is enormously important. That unique interaction may make a complete transition from negative to positive participation in your life."

-VERONICA

62

Spirit Guides IV
Reconnecting After Separation

"Many of you who aspire to connect with spirit feel the urgency deeply. When a disconnect is in motion the lack of energy flow feels devastating to those who remember it differently.

It is important to remain focused on the soulful part of yourself. Linear dramas and interference from outside sources often distort the energy needed to maintain or reconnect to spirit.

We recommend a selective quiet moment where your spirit guide may have opportunity to make its presence known. Assigning a scripted moment to this can cloud and confuse the probability even more.

Separate from the timeline if possible whenever you can. This will provide a moment of clarity that may produce an opportunity for dialogue with your guides. Understand your most previous interaction with them was most likely non-linear.

Leave all preconceived expectations behind. The submersion needed to be in linear can leave one unable to participate fully at first. It is through conscious focus and release that one may be able to reconnect to that eternal relationship.

No matter how evolved one may feel in the linear, it is always beneficial to reflect upon the basics of connection.

Linear dramas can become intense knocking even the most advanced energies off their base of inner knowing.

The renewal of connection to your guides is beneficial no matter how far you are on your path to evolvement."

-VERONICA

"Thinking makes stuff happen.

Knowing it early on makes all the difference..."

From: Ginno in "Parting Notes":
A Connection With The Afterlife

63

Eternal Plan

"It was never intended while in the linear to separate from the eternal viewpoint. As an energy evolved it was to participate fully with all aspects of the multiple experiences. This was to occur as the soul integrated more fully in the physical forms of choice... a condensed experience coupled with all experience so the soul energy involved could make choices based not only upon the current linear but layers of life experience.

In various cultures the perspective speaks to the eternal differently. The more advanced the energy, the more the layers came into conscious participation.

The history of your earth plane is far more diverse than has been imagined or discovered by the current measurement. The ancient cultures viewed are but a mere fraction of what has transpired on the physical stage you now participate in.

With each participation the souls involved became more adept at the integration. Ancient belief systems included the eternal perspective and plan. Each generation adds or subtracts according to the soul evolvement of the culture.

Often an energy will feel a lack or loss of meaning while examining a single linear life. It would rather be like reading one chapter of a novel then being expected to define the storyline... an interesting chapter but nonetheless incomplete.

All linear experiences build upon each other while working towards the soul's purpose. The eternal plan is based on many experiences. There are none who have had only one.

The soul's purpose is as diverse and different as the physical manifestations of the energies involved. Unique and driven the soul seeks the full story of its participation.

Not just one chapter."

-VERONICA

"Many of you who aspire to connect with spirit feel the urgency deeply..."

From: VERONICA

64

<u>The World of Now</u>

"The reality earth plane on which you currently exist is a result of the energy of your participation. In the time line each generation has left an imprint of positive and negative that has tipped quite vigorously into the negative. This is a result of being unconsciously without the influence of the soul.

Most will reply to this vehemently that they have participated religiously within the parameters of their linear consciousness... the spiritual influences being regulated by a confined perspective that places all spiritual power and creation to an outside source.

Our position is that bringing the soulful energy into the person can alter the imbalance that is occurring.

Generations of incarnated souls have been aligned to place the power of thought outside of themselves. The idea of a god being the omnipotent energy that decides the path of the physical beings that worship him.

Now that the planet's energy is dangerously askew we implore all souls incarnate to bring that omnipotent energy where it belongs, to the internal thought process by which all of you create reality (i.e. free will).

Your current linear is salvageable, however, the declaration of concentrated thought must be reclaimed so that the balance of energy can be regained. Free will is the claiming of the thought process that saves... so to speak... everything.

Do not feel the linear influence - "Oh I am but one."

All of you come from unique entity sources designed to bring a balance of perspective to your linear creation.

Participate energetically. Your connection to others may and will influence the mass consciousness creation that has gone awry.

Seize each day and bring your energy to it. It will make a difference. Think.

Be persistent. Be linear while expressing your eternal soul. It is why you are here.

Become the energy of your soul and all will be well.

What if you were the <u>one</u> soul needed to tip the balance to the more positive participation?"

-VERONICA

"Drink in all your lives.

Use the moments as an opportunity to evolve.

Each breath a gift.

Each deed a significant moment to who you are

and who you are to become."

From: Amos in "Parting Notes":
A Connection With The Afterlife

65

Past Lives

"Outside of the linear there dwells an infinity of experience that plays a part in your current physical existence. Since when you are born into most cultures you are taught and expected to consider only the current moment. This can sometimes be overwhelming.

It is, however, a fact. You have multiple lives that make up the "novel" of your linear participation. When not embodied you do have recall of the information. In body there are sometimes coincidental moments that often give one pause. Sometimes one can explain them away, however, often they remain an enigma to the current perspective.

So if there are incidents that feel incomplete or out of sync with your life, it may be that it is an episode in the grander picture of your existence. These incidents often may make perfect sense in a full perspective of your multiple incarnating.

Opening the mind to such a possibility can give clarity to the confusing moments while defining who you are as a soul, not the personality you are manifesting as in this life.

An advanced soul will often have several thousand experiences to draw upon while engaging a lesson or plan. Multiple lives are a tool to the soul's evolution."

-VERONICA

66

<u>Timeline</u>

"It is beneficial while physical to recognize and separate from the conscious perception of time whenever one is able.

Physical life needs the timeline to define and understand the progression of the body. In actuality the physical form was designed to last at least 200 of your earth years... the system easily regenerating itself through positive thought.

The distractions in focus combined with the toxins created through neglect and improper use have limited most lives to less than 100 years. This ironically is perceived as an improvement in your more recent moments.

Before the most recent historical documentation the life spans were more easily lengthened. (We are speaking of Atlantis and Lemuria.) A shift in perception and aligning resulted in more disease and difficulty for spirit to manifest in physical biological form.

There is at this time, opportunity for energy shifts and expansions that some have identified as a linear 2012. We say yes there is a shift but the linear timeline is rather irrelevant.

Energy is regaining its foothold upon the idea of biology in your sphere of reality. There is an expansion that will transcend time as you know it.

We advise adherence to non-linear perceptions whenever possible. It is the swiftest path to evolution, especially if you are linear.

Calm the chaos, silence the chatter. Become one with your energy that is timeless. Then and only then will there be unification with your participation in this timeline. Seek the silence."

-VERONICA

"You need to know who you are...

You need to know what you want...

...And be truthful about both of them."

From: VERONICA

67

Times of Trouble

"In all linear experiences there are moments that bring imbalance and confusion to the individual. In the attempt to right this predicament the incarnate soul begins to investigate the physical life to find clarity and solution.

We speak to many who are disheartened by the inability of the physical psyche to right the perceived imbalance: Each attempt seemingly creating more confusion and distinct feeling of loss.

In these times of trouble the only hope for solution is the immersion back to the soul energy... a separation from the dramas that appear larger than life itself.

We suggest that a reconnection to that soul energy in a calm confident way will lead to alignment of your physical participation.

Times of trouble may be difficult and uncomfortable but provide an opportunity to realign the spiritual path that you and your soul are engaging.

As in all things linear, it will be perceived as a length of time until "all" appears aligned but it will occur.

Return to your soul the powerful seed of who you are.

Abandon the distractions of drama.

One may do this immediately and thoroughly with focus.

Return to your soul in times of trouble. It is truly the only solution."

                                        -VERONICA

68

<u>Mass Consciousness</u>

"In the physical there is the reality created by the individual soul... and the mass consciousness event... which is a combined created reality often associated with culture.

Most of you live in a culture that is extremely volatile for a myriad of reasons. As a single soul these events can cause a sense of unbalance and helplessness. It feels rather like a wave of negativity rushing towards you in often a personal way.

One mutters to the self about the inexplicable feeling of overwhelming emotion as one feels victim to this combined energy.

It is clearly a disturbing event as one falls prey to the combined positive but often predominantly negative mass consciousness event.

How does one separate from such energy?

It is possible even in the face of great combined adversity. Mass consciousness is indeed a mixture of all the individual thoughts of souls incarnate. To change a free fall of events during these times it is important for each individual soul to take responsibility for themselves and align their own personal thoughts to a more positive venue.

Each of you is now assessing your individual energy in the current mass event.

If there are a thousand souls willing to connect with their higher power and align their thoughts there is opportunity for a change of venue.

The important thing is to remember the importance and power of your soul in connection with All That Is.

Each individual soul is a part of the mass consciousness. If all of you regain your focus it is possible to change the mass consciousness outcome.

By considering this, you empower yourself and your culture."

-VERONICA

"I am happy. My fear was unfounded..."

From: Raymond in "Parting Notes":
A Connection with the Afterlife

69

<u>Despair</u>

"As one participates in life there are moments where the individual feels helpless navigating through all the dramas. The spiraling effect of choices by the ego can place one in a fragile position often defined a despair.

Despair from a spiritual definition is where a consciousness chooses its self into a corner where no matter what decision is made, the end result is non-movement in the soul's evolution.

This can trickle back to the linear moment as a paralysis of sorts for the soul & the linear self. The ego, not sure what to decide, becomes agitated with the end result... negative beyond the comprehension of the physical self.

What to do?

A return to the soulful moments are imperative. By placing a value upon the energy of the self rather than the perceived actor in place there is opportunity for a renewal of energy.

It is important to stop the negative thoughts through meditation or another physical/soulful process. There are no standard processes as each of you are unique representations of your soul.

Look despair in the face & consciously decide to make different choices. It will not be easy. Many linear (inappropriate) things will fall away. The goal is to jump start the soul energy. By doing so a new creative opportunity will become available.

Let it go."

-VERONICA

70

<u>Growing Up</u>

"Often as a child in the physical world one is asked, 'What do you want to be when you grow up'?

The answers vary from child to child as their years advance for each of those children. It is a typical question asked of various cultures, each one with its parameters & definitions.

We ask, however, how many of you ask of yourselves what you will be if your soul learns all of its proposed lessons and essentially grows up?

We realize there is a concept of soulful growth but it is often intertwined with a religious moment or a concept outdated by advancement not perceived by the linear self.

In the timeline the idea of goal changes as the child develops and considers new ideas & opportunities. What one ascribed to at age 8 usually aligns differently by the age of 18. At 28 all of those thoughts may be replaced by ones never considered by the teenager or the child.

Thus it is for the soul.

You are ever evolving. The idea of clinging to concepts out dated by your advancement seems ridiculous in print. However, there are a number of you who do so out of obligation and/or tradition.

As you feel yourself 'growing up' spiritually it is important to consider the progress of your soul and what is necessary to maintain it in the linear.

Releasing concepts no longer relevant to the soul is imperative. It is not perhaps turning away from 'God', but actually turning inward to the self & soul, the ultimate manifestation of 'God'."

-VERONICA

"Love is an expression of connection without any conditions..."

From : VERONICA

71

Artful Expression of the Soul

"The linear physical existence is a canvas of opportunity for those who are vivid, colorful artists. Nowhere in "All That Is" can a soul express itself so emotionally & thought filled.

It is important for all of you to take to your heart this incredible gift of creation. The current timeline distracts from expression of the soul with the perceived imbalance of energy. All of you have created artfully a linear hero to deliver you from your miscalculated efforts of creation.

It is often that way in the physical.

Your history provides many variations of an energetic hero focused upon deliverance. This time is no different.

We would caution the importance of your continued participation, and not lending all your focus to someone else creating your reality.

Be a full participant in this resolving moment. It is only the illusion of a messiah that intrigues the linear you. If you must, use the illusion to regain your confidence but realize that reality, especially mass consciousness events, requires the thoughtful artful expression of all.

Do not sit back & wait for deliverance. Be an artful expressive energy in the creation of the event."

-VERONICA

72

Forgiveness

"Most all have been impacted by negative experiences. Often the transgressors are those we hold most dear.

The heart aches in reaction to displays of multi-tiered abuses that are enacted while in a linear life.

Some may say that these experiences tend to accelerate in the course of a life. The crescendo of betrayal, abandonment, cruelty, emotional trauma, etc. leaves the soul feeling bruised and weak.

One can succumb to these negative moments... or forgive them.

Forgive?

We can feel the soul energy questioning the word energetically. Some tend to cling to the "bad" experiences in life prohibiting their own evolution in the process.

Not all souls are evolved enough to even realize they have offended. So it is for the more aware soul to find a path of forgiveness for those who participate negatively towards them.

The idea of evolving may be actually an opportunity to see clearly those who have offended and realize they are merely inept in their participation.

Forgiveness can allow the evolving process to begin for both parties.

We realize that it may be difficult for those in the "now" of your current linear as the process can be a multiple life experience.

We, however, still encourage the forgiveness moment for all who are in linear.

It is the best way to evolve as we see it. All of those who have offended may not be as great as yourself, but self forgiveness is often the most difficult to achieve."

-VERONICA

"The goal of the soul is for you to become aligned with your entity's intent...."

From: VERONICA

73

Reincarnational Process

"Many have written to us about the idea of their reincarnational process. It is important for all souls to perceive the value of such a system... each life a gift that constructs the soul's participation in the linear.

Since the soul is eternal it is necessary for the dense linear experience to be multifaceted. This is defined by the concept that not every life will be easy or pleasant.

We have been queried about these more difficult lives as to why they are necessary. Certainly incarnating into misery should be eliminated from the process... or should they?

If one truly adheres to a nonphysical multidimensional process, the need for a full rounded "look" at <u>all</u> aspects of a linear life is paramount to the evolution of the soul. Since that is precisely the root of the physical participation, it is a moment that truly cannot be eliminated from the full experience.

We realize while in the physical form it is quite common to establish a belief system that can single out the current life as the total and full experience. Many have expressed a desire to stop the reincarnational process because they feel it's either unnecessary or too difficult to continue.

The "personality" may decide from its singular view that the experience is too harsh or unhelpful to achieve union with its higher entity. We suggest that once out of the dense linear experience most energies change that viewpoint by observing the full picture.

Be mindful that we are not diminishing the perspective of the eternal soul in a more unpleasant linear. We often counsel personalities how to better understand their situations and perhaps create the moment of ease that they seek.

We merely offer perspective of the process as a whole so that the desired evolution of the soul may be achieved.

Be assured that if once out of physical form you truly desire to no longer incarnate, it can and will be created by your consciousness.

We only advise to be aware of the perspective offered by the denseness of linear existence, especially all of the viewpoints, both positive and negative.

Both are required for a full evolution of your soul... which is why you are there."

-VERONICA

**"Security is being at peace
with one's self identity..."**

From: The Reflections of a Spiritual Astronaut Books

74

<u>Remember Who You Are</u>

"In the early mist of your soul's creation the concept of evolution soon began beating in a physical heart.

Taking form to participate was intended to bring expansion and clarity to your energy.

However, the dramas created for learning had the ability to increase without complete resolution.

Thus the majestic light of your soul's creativity became distorted or forgotten in the linear experience.

Every soul vibrates with a pulse that simmers in your sub consciousness awaiting release.

It surfaces sweetly like a whisper of thought wishing to tumble off the tip of your tongue but never quite arriving.

This often leads to frustration as you attempt to remember what you are seemingly forgetting to do in this life.

"What is my purpose?"

"Why am I here?"

Questions that speak loudly while the answers retreat into more meaningless dramas. The desire to the soul to speak becomes louder in your head until your heart explodes in its need to express its magnificent energy.

The soul, even when enduring physical suppression has the ability to expand.

Often the largest opponent to this expansion is the physical belief system that is in place.

It is important to remember that no matter what has occurred in your life, the soul's intention is to shine its light forth.

Release the perceived mistakes and supposed wrong turns.

Embrace your creativity while weaving through that maze of unfortunate dramas.

You and your soul have the ability to do so.

You will prevail.

Leave the darkness of despair and let the light of who your are shine through.

It will make a difference.

Remember not only your physical self but who you are as a soul. It's all within you awaiting your return & focus."

-VERONICA

75

The Big Picture

"In the beginning the recently cast soul anticipates the coming physical moment with the feeling of promise and expansion.

The goals in place, it proceeds to the linear plane with enthusiasm, while extending itself to the experience.

The physical reality is intense as the soul struggles to maneuver through the sign posts and evolvements. Often the life ends too quickly as some error of judgment ends the physical experience prematurely.

Undaunted, the soul re-enters the physical plane again, perhaps without the contemplation necessary for more productive experiences... the cycle often escalating until a pattern of repetition impedes the soul's development.

The physical personality is left with a spinning perspective of the lessons involved until to maintain its balance, it perceives only the dramas at hand.

It is important to realize that recognized drama can be realigned or eliminated. Stepping back from the linear's intense focus to the larger picture can give clarity.

This big picture focus offers an opportunity to find solutions while maintaining the physical focus.

Step back.

Realign your focus.

See everything, not just the explosive drama in front of you.

The solution will be easier to see in the big picture.

Step back.

Re-Focus.

Align.

The big picture may offer more answers of resolution, and your soul perceiving all the energy will have opportunity to assist.

Step back.

See the bigger picture."

-VERONICA

"Change can only occur with the full cooperation of mind, body, and spirit..."

From: The Reflections of a Spiritual Astronaut Books

76

<u>Encouragement</u>

"The days blend into a stream of monotony for those souls struggling to evolve.

Patterns repeat themselves causing the more advanced to cry in frustration while the younger energies become confused.

A sense of isolation created by the physical environment can lead to dismal perspective.

If you find yourself at the end of your tether remember this......

Your spiritual perspective can ease you through the difficult times. When encountering difficulties your soul may ease the loneliness and give you clarity.

You are never alone.

Your guides are ever present to comfort you.

Know that they are there, and that your soul embraces the attention they give. The difficulty arises when the physical experience blocks the spiritual one.

Know that there is always a probable moment that will relieve the tension your are feeling.

Reach out to it..... let the soul guide you to a redeeming moment in the now.

You can do it.

Spirit is reaching towards you.

All that is needed is for you to extend yourself to it.

Go ahead.

It *is* possible."

-VERONICA

**"There are areas of your soul
that you have not even acknowledged yet..."**

From: VERONICA

77

<u>Lamenting the Past</u>

"In your now the future holds a flame of promise. It flickers in front of you while beckoning the soul to move towards it in hope.

Most are able to maneuver towards their next experience due to that now moment.

Often in life one becomes less likely to be able to evolve to that future. The past in all its forms can be a great distraction to those seeking advancement.

Often your days are filled with lamentations of... "I could have done that better."... "What was I thinking in that decision?" Etc...

It is important to realize that the past is just that.... past. In a linear forum you cannot change it.

In a spiritual venue one can shift the energy experience into a positive current moment so that your future creations are not compromised by your past.

The balance between the past and self is not easily defined by verbiage. It can only be felt in the depths of your soul.

Release the past and FEEL the future while existing in the NOW."

-VERONICA

78

A Return to the Soul

"Often while physical the external stimulus of the environment can become difficult and disappointing. Many assign blame to circumstances [which seem]... apparently to them... out of their control.

By playing the part of victim there appears to be a tolerance to a seemingly endless parade of mishaps. The events can escalate to even more intolerable scenarios until the physical incarnate becomes overwhelmed.

When "bad times" persist, it is important not to give power to external manifestations.

A thoughtful reckoning internally may be the key to more productive moments.

Your physical being is but a product of your soul. To change what is externally created one must reach to the inner core of the self to find peace and clarity.

Daily dramas can distract even the most advanced of souls. If you find yourself in an undesirable predicament remember this: what is occurring is coming from your energy. To stop it one must reach deep within to alter the vibration that created the situation.

It takes courage to do so. It's never easy, however, extremely rewarding if successful.

Your physical self will have difficulties realigning your creative energy to stop the march of unfortunate incidents. This is the importance of going back internally to the soul. It is eternal.

Remember that the physical world around you is but one of many you have experienced. It will dissolve into memory while your soul moves towards evolution.

Return to the soul.

It is your greatest refuge.

It is your connection to the source of All That Is.

Return."

-VERONICA

"Self forgiveness is often the most difficult to achieve..."

From: VERONICA

79

Timelessness

"We are often asked how to connect with one's own soul. In your culture it is often a tedious task. The reason has its roots in the measurement of time.

Outside of the linear time is not a consideration. The eternal moment... which is ever in the present...is the only constant.

We suggest for those wishing to connect with their higher vibration, that a separation from the timeline would be beneficial.

The soul reflects without the chaos of the dramatic timeline with ease. An opportunity to step out of the timeline is a wondrous experience for those desiring connection.

A suggestion of a period of time where time is not considered, can be a wonderful reconnection to the soul.

Perhaps a weekend of no clocks, no measurement and no participation in time whatsoever... the soul in its natural timeless state while living as human as possible.

Reflecting on one's participation in a physical environment while appreciating its spiritual gifts. Ah! What a true gift that would be.

So dear friend...... be bold..... step out of physical time....... allow the timelessness of the soul to participate with your human experience.

Your perspective will expand, allowing the full integration of mind, body, and soul.

Take the steps necessary to be timeless for a few sun ups and sun downs. It may change how you proceed from where you are.

Be eternal for a moment.

You may be surprised at the powerfulness of it all."

-VERONICA

"There is a vast space waiting for each person... waiting to be molded into something of your choosing. The best way to prepare is to practice creating what you want *there*."

From: Tessie in "Parting Notes":
A Connection with the Afterlife"

80

<u>Be Not Afraid....</u>

"Physical reality is a dense energetic opportunity for the soul's expansion.

Not all of it is pretty, not all of it is easy to comprehend. However, the moments offered are a perspective that is not so available in the spiritual realm.

Seek the expression boldly, as you have created it for your own purpose. Your actions in difficulty offer a window to who you are.

Be not afraid as you are not alone in all the trials and tribulations. Dig deep into your energy to find the purpose of your soul while embracing the lesson that has been created to serve your energy.

Feel the hand of your entity as it brushes away the tear from your eye. Know that all who love you are encircling you with their love.

Be not afraid. It does not serve the moment. Be connected to your soul who has created your life. Know that you are not alone. Feel the warmth and let it embrace your heart.

The hurt will subside in the connection. You are treasured by all those who love you in spirit.

Rejoice in that feeling and be not afraid. In fact be quite the opposite.....<u>Bold</u>."

-VERONICA

81

Remember Who You are

"Well, most of you become fearful when you feel powerless, when you allow other energies to intersect with yours that diminish who you are as a soul.

To adhere to that type of thought process is extremely damaging. You must remember who you are. You must remember that you are an omnipotent energy. You have the God source within your heart, here (she gestures). Use that. Do not allow yourself to become diminished by any sort of outside energy.

Reach down into the depths of you and bring forth your Godlike energy and understand that you can overcome anything. If something is in your path that has caused you to feel diminished, take a good look at it, and use your soulful energy to diminish it away from you. Do not become victim to anything that is thrown at you.

Realize who you are; realize that your soul energy can come forth with you and fix everything. But, you have to believe and you have to connect with the Godlike energy that is within you. Do not allow outside forces to diminish you ever.

And, when you are at your worst, that is the best time to reach and pull out your soulful energy and change the course of what you perceive is your path. Never, ever doubt your connection with the Godlike energy within you. It is there, it is available - just get it. And you can do this. And you can rise above any difficulty. Spirit is with you, always."

-VERONICA

82

<u>You Are The Artist of Your Life</u>

"Well, one often feels victim to their linear life. They feel that perhaps things are being created that they follow rather than what they create. They say that "I am at the receiving end of the energy" and we think that perhaps some of them have been brought up to believe that structure, that they are at the receiving end of a higher power that is designing their life, and if it comes up a little bit difficult, well then, one must suffer through it.

We'd say that it is important for all of you to understand that you are the artists of your life. Your life is a canvas. It is created by you, the parameters are set up by you, and whatever you want to paint, you can paint.

There's not a free moment where it is designed and you are just following the numbers and coloring in what is going to occur. It is actually you drawing, deciding, contouring what it is you are going to paint. And then you spend the whole lifetime bringing in textures of color, mixtures of color that bring new nuances to the moment that you might not have ever considered before.

Life isn't a paint-by-number. Life is an artistic creation by your soul, and you are the master artist in this regard."

-VERONICA

83

Create......
(To "Stick" or be "Un-Stuck")

"Your soul, infinite in its existence, chooses physical reality as an opportunity to participate in creation. All spiritual energy feels the desire of expression whether in nonphysical or physical. The level of participation may vary but ultimately that creative process aligns your soul, enhancing its connection with all that vibrates in reality.

So, if you are feeling stuck in your focus being an omnipotent energy in a physical form.... create... anything..... Bring forth a part of your soul no matter how simplistic it may feel.

Allow your soulful energy to unfurl itself while igniting your thoughts creatively to bring in a spiritual creation to this reality.

This alignment not only will be a fulfillment to your dimension but will also move stagnant energy within you.... This allowing will bring better manifestation to your reality.

The feeling of being stuck may dissipate giving you a chance to reconnect with physical & yourself.

Create what, you ask.

The answer lies between a simple endeavor to a complex one. It's your energy that will define it. Breathe new life into your self and ride the wave of creative power that is within all of you.

It may be dulled from inappropriate outside influence but indeed it is still there. Reach down deeply and reconnect to whatever your soul resonates with.

It will make a difference.

Creation is the fuel of the soul & its expression."

-VERONICA

"Your deepest fear is not that you are unable to manifest... but that you can.... and simply did not attempt it with enough boldness..."

From: VERONICA

84

<u>Defining Yourself</u>

"Incarnating into a physical reality takes great focus and courage. An energy like your Self having the gift of free will moves though the experience through choices made. The harshness of the physical combined with the free will of others may leave one feeling overwhelmed and powerless.

Since the only real control is that of yourself, it is important to define it. This knowing enables more stability from an internal perspective, leaving the rest of the outside interaction less of an influence.

Take time to perceive the inner core of your essence. Let go of the routine of life whenever you can. Glide into the space where its just your soul. All of the drama around you will subside if you do so.

Change how you interact with others and your environment. It could be one small gesture from you that ripples through it all and heals it.

You are the creator of your reality. Define the "you" in all of it and the rest will align with more integrity.

Know yourself, but better yet define the you of this life."

-VERONICA

85

<u>You Are Never Alone</u>

"Many souls when separating from Source to experience the linear environment feel a sense of aloneness that is difficult to overcome. Compounded by dramas, the feeling of isolation can leave one feeling powerless in the seeming vastness of the physical timeline.

To have the dense experience the sense of singularity is strong within the psyche of the incarnate. It does not, however, have to be exclusive from the soul's participation. It is possible to have the physical, hand in hand with the comfort of your soul.

The entity from which you come is always present in your energy. It is possible to focus in the linear while being interwoven in the fabric of your soul.

Attempt to reach within yourself to make the connection. Your energy will reach back to you in response to your loneliness. It was always there and it wishes for your awareness of the connection.

You are never alone. It is only the perception of separateness that confuses you. Reach for your soul. It's already extended to you.

Even now.

Go ahead.

You will not be disappointed.

Reach.

Reach within."

-VERONICA

86

"Anger"

"In physical reality one not only engages the thought process, one also encounters emotion. One of them is Anger.

This state of consciousness arrives spontaneously rather than through conscious planning. Many identify it as a negative response to situations where one has a sense of powerlessness.

Still others define it as a response of displeasure to a situation, or being wronged by another.

In older times the word originated from "angr", which meant sorrow or grief. We tend to embrace this definition as it signifies the true energy of the emotion.

To become angry is actually a healthy response to something that brings us sorrow. Instead of crying one responds with anger feeling that it is a more powerful counter to the feelings of grief.

Spirit encourages all emotion including anger. The sorrow one feels escalates to anger when one feels defenseless in a situation. It is an armor all wear when confronted with grief.

It is a natural response, however, often it is held onto for longer than it should be. Anger not released can become toxic.

It can cloud one's thought process, not allowing for reconciliation.

It is important to let anger go.

Whatever it was prompted by has come and gone. The feelings of anger, however, can linger long and decrease the ability to evolve.

Be angry, but then let it go.

The path to spirit does not require you take it with you.

It is an emotion and a tool created to enhance the experience.

Use it then release it.

Your soul will thank you."

-VERONICA

"You are never alone.

Your guides are ever present to comfort you."

From: VERONICA

87

You and the Planet

We have been asked to comment on the stability of your environment. It is always a volatile experience living upon a sphere in the physical. One must always keep in mind that the planet is a conscious being just as you are.

It is constantly shifting and evolving while making expanding choices for its energy. Of course it is not the same experience as yours but energetically compatible in many ways.

The confusion of this current environment has impacted all, including this earth. It is important at this time to meet the volatile energy and attempt to soothe it. This can be accomplished by treating yourself and others kindly.

The energy will trickle into the soul of the planet and realign it, while also realigning yourselves.

It is a partnership this experience. The more you understand that the better the planet will realign and become more tranquil. You are reflections of each other. One pattern extends from both of you....... the planet and you.

Realize that the interweaving of the experience is rather like a cooperative that has impact both soulfully and physically for all.

Start with yourself. If each of you reaches for their energy, it will impact the earthly plane. Becoming one is the only path to take. Treat the earth as you would treat a loved one.

This change of energy will make a difference.

It's worth the effort.

Do it."

-VERONICA

"Your physical being is but a product of your soul.

To change what is externally created one must reach to the inner core of the self to find peace and clarity..."

From: VERONICA

88

Boundaries

(Release Them)

"In the progress of the soul the ideas formed are limitless. Each incarnation offers another opportunity to experience and evolve.

If one finds themself confined or stagnated by boundaries, it is important to explore the roots of those limitations. The soul ever seeks full exploration. The physical participation often feels the energy of past experience or current creations as limits to what the soul can truly create.

Letting go of disappointment, feelings of worthlessness, and general lack of promise is important.

Remember it was not your intent as a soul to limit yourself. Do not let negative participation create boundaries that you feel are insurmountable. It is the perception of the ego that cultivates that perspective.

Let go as much as you are able of the boundaries that bind you to a circumstance that no longer serves the evolution of your soul.

Release.

Breathe and let it go.

You are a powerful energy having a linear experience. Reattach to your soul, push past the boundaries you have created.

You are able to do so, since you created them to begin with.

Take down the walls and reunite with your self.

A limitless incarnation has much to offer if you will allow yourself to receive it.

Release.

Take down the boundaries.

From there the probabilities are endless.

Go ahead.

Release."

-VERONICA

"We suggest for those wishing to connect with their higher vibration, that a separation from the timeline would be beneficial..."

From VERONICA

89

The Oasis of Your Soul

"Traveling through the physical environment there are many twists and turns that can lead to many destinations. Intersections with others can lead one to moments where one feels lost and desolate, a rather desert of reality.

In times of lack the only recourse is to return to the energy of who you are, which is the soul.

Within this infinite energy the elixir of life resides... its nurturing moment providing an opportunity to replenish that which seems to be taken from you.

Feel the cooling properties that quench the thirst for peace. A tranquil breath of fresh air that can only be inhaled by the soul.

All of it can translate to your physical reality if you let it.

We caution that immediate relief may take some time as it trickles back to you. However, never doubt that the oasis of the soul in a desert environment is never far off. It is a real moment not a mirage. Believe in the solid energy as it releases all the discomfort.

It is your choice so make it.

The oasis is inviting and it is real.

Decide to be there or not. A moment of respite before returning is well needed. The journey can indeed be treacherous, but if one resides soulfully in the oasis the journey can be easier."

-VERONICA

90

The Importance of Living In Your Truth

"While experiencing the linear plane there are many opportunities to express your Self fully. Your soul was created in absolute truth in the bosom of your entity. Springing forth to gather experience in the physical there are many moments where ones' truth may be diluted through the posturing and dramas of others.

We caution giving in to the easy moment. Regardless of the drama one must remain true to the essence of your energy. Anyone who would create it otherwise does not have your best interests at heart.

The intersection of others can leave you scrambling to regain your center. It is important to consider remaining firm in the resolve to be aligned with your soul. Do not allow others to deter you from that path.

Calm yourself daily with the resolve to be connected. Back up from relationships and dramatics that would result in confusion.

Remember that there is no confusion in your soul. It is only your linear self that may be distracted from what is appropriate for you.

We understand the complexity of physical and how one can become so disconnected. However, it is your responsibility to regain the relationship with yourself.

Decide.

then........

Act accordingly.

Stay in the energy that you know deep down defines you.

It is the only way to regain your ability to be in your truth."

-VERONICA

"If you haven't guessed,

I'll give you a clue,

the master of the universe,

is inside of you..."

From: The Reflections of a Spiritual Astronaut Books

91

<u>Healing</u>

"Incarnating into the physical environment is a courageous thing. With free will in place anything can and will occur to the soul who places themselves within the environment.

Dramas unfold hoping to beckon growth... the soul moving through the lesson with as much vigor as possible. It should occur with greatness as knowledge and understanding allow expansion. However, that is often not the case as damage arises while interacting with others who may be reacting instead of acting to the evolution of the soul.

In these moments the heart may feel wounded as others may have created abrasive scenarios that one who has agreed to the lesson must endure. The best plans of the soul do not always unfold with ease.

The wounding may last for lifetimes but often it is available for a healing moment. If you have been through such a drama it is important to allow yourself the space to heal. In the linear this may happen on its own but there are conscious opportunities to allow healing to occur.

Close your eyes and sense the pulse of your soul as it inhabits the form. As your heart beats, feel the soothing nature of spirit. Attempt to find a place of forgiveness so that the open wound will stop hurting.

Often the others in the drama may not be at the same stage of evolution as you are. In these moments understand that they will continue the drama but you do not have to if you so desire.

Choose to be free of it and allow yourself to let go of the dialogue that is wounding you.

Release it spiritually...

... then...

Release it emotionally...

... then...

Release yourself from the bonds of the physical encounter.

They will catch up with you when they have evolved. It is time for you to heal.... and continue your growth.

It is alright to do so.

Your healing is the most importing thing now.

Give yourself permission to do so."

-VERONICA

"It is no longer a time for tears... but a time for Action."

From: VERONICA

92

The Positive Evolution of Your Soul

"The linear life is seeded with opportunity as it unfolds. Experiences arise, relationships are created, and a reality is set into motion as one lives the life.

In the youthful times choices made often return to haunt as the soul ages in the body. Memories of choices often intrude upon the present, causing emotional regrets. It is important to balance these thoughts with the notion that they have led you to where you are now.

If you feel that the choices left you in a negative present, the only way to proceed is to forgive yourself. By doing so you leave yourself in a now to create future experiences in a more suitable fashion.

Regardless of where your choices leave you, regretting does nothing to help you create the present moment. You cannot alter the past to color the now. Be your full soul now no matter what has preceded the moment.

It is the only way to continue towards positive evolution of the soul."

-VERONICA

93

Unconditional Love

"Many teachers speak of the power of unconditional love for others. It is proposed as the enlightened way of reality. There is much truth in this practice throughout the physical existence. The ability to love without condition is an enlightened path that many aspire to live by.

We agree.

However, we would also include the unconditional love of the self, which is often misconstrued as ego.

Going through a physical incarnation requires a boldness that is unmatched in other perspectives. Thoughts as one proceeds often do not include unconditional love. But perhaps the opposite.... judgment.

If you find yourself in judgment of the self, it would be a correct move to also consider the love of self.

It is a huge ingredient in the evolution of the soul. For without it one may wander aimlessly throughout many lifetimes.

Appreciate the tenacity needed to maneuver through a lifetime. Incorrect choices and downright mistakes thrive within a physical moment. It is the ability to love yourself regardless that is the key to advancement.

So perhaps the elimination of the strict regimen one has prescribed for the self might be in order.

Look a yourself as a wondrous creation. Realize that choices and paths are just that and do not define you as a soul.

Errors in judgment should leave room for the idea that you are deserving of self love no matter what the circumstances.

By practicing self love you give yourself permission to be less than perfect on your quest to enlightenment.

It is definitely something to consider."

-VERONICA

"Be connected to your soul,

who has created your life.

Know that you are not alone.

Feel the warmth and let it embrace your heart..."

From: VERONICA

94

<u>Finding The Hope Within You</u>

"Often in a life one can find a moment where all the energy of creation feels like a void inside. Despair over predicaments and dramas can lead to the inability to create anything productive in a linear sense.

In times of troublesome mass consciousness the individual may simply run out of hope for a better creation with the life.

Dramas can cause blindness to the true capabilities of the soul. Each moment unfolding feeling worse than the last. It is easy to be overwhelmed with the negativity and just give up.

By doing so one merely reinforces the sense of defeat. When one believes they are overcome they will be.

By remaining steadfast to your soulful energy one can regain the hope within and overcome anything.

Be one with your soul choosing to ignore the mass energy that can become overpowering in its negativity.

Instead of getting in the mix of defeat, attempt to break out of the crowd and become individual with your thoughts. One does not have to follow the mass moments of consciousness. One is capable of creating their own stream if they are willing to be bold and just do it.

We realize how intricate physical reality is created. We also know how difficult it is to attempt to break out of the mold and be different. This is especially so at this time in your culture.

Reinvent how you think about yourself and your surroundings. Attempt to change thought patterns that have gotten you to where you are now. Somewhere deep down your hope still exists. Do not allow the exterior to rule the interior of you.

Dig deep and find yourself. Regain your grip on hope. It is a special ingredient in your reality. Add it to your thoughts and allow it to regain its foothold within you."

-VERONICA

"It is important to view all those who would interact into your life with clarity. View each as an ingredient that should add substance and vitality to your world, not distract from it..."

From: VERONICA

95

<u>When You Leave This Life</u>

"It is important to realize that all of your experiences in the physical contribute to your evolution. <u>When you leave this life</u> you will consider what went well and what didn't.

However, it is but one life in a long line of experience for most of you. One must consider all of the lives when deciding how to proceed.

A time of contemplation emerges from the infinite, so that while with your guides one can determine the next best course of action.

All is considered carefully in preparation for what is appropriate for your soul's evolution.

Often when while still in a life there can be distortion to what is actually in your best interest. Emotional response to your actions and actions of others can lead to distress. This often hinders clear choice making. To remedy these moments it is important to see the full picture of all your existences so that decisions may be made more clearly.

Slow down.

Attempt to rise to the viewpoint of multiple lives and their importance in the big picture.

It is not necessary to judge yourself by this one life. Expand your thoughts to include everything. It will ease your suffering and perhaps enable you to put all of the pieces of the puzzle together.

After the singular perspective has been taught to you, one should consider other lives to better understand the one you are in.

Your soul wishes to evolve. The complexity of your energy could simply not expand in only one try. Open your thoughts to the eternal perspective. It will help you define your progression.

After all, it is all about the progress of the soul towards evolution.

Consider it.

You will feel better."

-VERONICA

**"Dramas can cause blindness
to the true capabilities of the soul..."**

From: VERONICA

96

Connecting To Your Soul

"If one were to stay always in the eternal one would never comprehend the definition of the linear self or the soul.

Becoming human is complicated on many levels. The soul wishes to evolve but the condition of physical often hinders the idea of the true self.

Defining the self while connecting to the soul is a powerful moment. It is important to remember that you are truly the only one who can define your purpose and its energy.

Spirit may be able to guide you to the right arenas but ultimately it is you who must take the final steps.

Always meet your soul head on with all the energy you can muster. There are no conditions from your soul, it is completely unconditional in its desire to connect with you.

Let go of all outside definitions given to you by others. This is an intimate moment with your soulful energy. Never allow anyone to define you from the outside. Your soul is inside and has the ability to shine through you in this physical reality.

Keep the intimacy of soul and define yourself by it.

All answers lie within.

Define yourself by becoming one with your energy.

It is the correct path.

Just follow it."

                                        -VERONICA

"Free will is the claiming of the thought process..."

From: VERONICA

"There is no better company
than the higher aspects of yourself..."

From: VERONICA

97

<u>Recipes For Evolvement</u>

"Being physical is a challenge for all souls. The thickness of the energetic environment may wreak havoc upon those who wish to evolve. Without clear thoughts one may beckon many energies into the field of their participation creating a recipe of difficulty.

It is important to view all those who would interact into your life with clarity. View each as an ingredient that should add substance and vitality to your world, not distract from it.

Often it becomes necessary to review negative participation and eliminate them from your realm. It is never an easy thing to do, as some are familiar signposts in your life.

When desiring evolution, those who would not be conducive to that path often need to be reassigned to their own moments so that the flow of your path is not impeded.

Look not at it as an elimination but rather more as of a "time out". Familiar energy that has become toxic could be the key ingredient to troublesome times for your own evolution.

Be brave in these moments. By moving the energy you create opportunity for expansion. Those who have blended in your environment who are toxic often are not aware of it.

You are the only one who may do all of you some good. Do not be afraid to eliminate an ingredient that no longer serves the recipe.

Often the ingredient merely needs a new environment.

Be brave.

Move the energy.

Evolve."

-VERONICA

"Remain Bold. It suits your true self..."

From: VERONICA

98

<u>This Happens Often In A Life</u>

"The Calm thinking needed to engage and respond to your reality is compromised by the chatter in your head. It becomes so loud that you are unable to listen to what's being said by your soul.

In an attempt to find clarity you search for the strength to break through to your soul. Frustration can mount when it's not easy and your emotions boil over to release some of the pressure. Yes. It can feel like too much with no end in sight. Isolated you despair, becoming more aligned with the chatter than anything else.

It's difficult to think clearly during these times. If indeed your thoughts create your reality then how does one recover from the chaos to better moments?

You have a choice now to either choose the chatter or to realign with the power of your soul. Use your emotions to break through to it. The soul is ever faithful. It can calm the chaos, soothe the heart, and turn off the chatter.

Your physical reality will not magically transform, however, the negative symptoms will start to dissipate.

Signs of hope are there but will need some moments to materialize.

In the meantime rejoice in the reunion, enjoy the clarity. Be patient as you heal so that you never return to that space of chaos again.

Go on.

Break Through.

Your soul awaits."

-VERONICA

"When was the last time you made a really bold move with your life?"

From: VERONICA

99

A Life Truly Blessed

"We have often listened to many in your culture that are extremely focused on riches and fame. We realize that it is indeed important to be able to function well in the linear. Basic needs have a cost in the everyday life and without money it is always a difficult process.

It is important to look at reality as a "give and take" of energy exchange. To receive energy you need to give energy. The integrity of your self while doing so defines the physical life.

The soul evolves through experience and your life provides that through various lessons that help advance the soul. Not all of them are easy.

Your thoughts are a power that drives your experience through the linear. Keeping your thoughts positive help in that regard. A constant focus on what you don't have can hinder prosperity even more.

A sense of gratitude for what does manifest can keep you on track. In other words focus on the progress while creating yourself towards the goal.

Give your energy fully regardless of what is received back. Initially you may be working through karmic energy or balancing an imbalance within yourself that makes it feel that the goal is unattainable.

Gratitude for what you do have is important. The thought structure will put you in a place of receiving the energy more freely. Comparison to others is inappropriate. Everyone creates different struggles for themselves.

We realize how difficult living a physical life may be. The twists and turns can deflate even the most healthy ego.

Know that in the end it won't be the riches or the fame you take with you. It will be the love and the energy exchange.

Appreciate what you have and perhaps the rest will follow. As for fame.... all of you are famous in the eye of your source energy."

-VERONICA

**"Once you can see past the drama in any situation,
you can usually overcome it..."**

From: VERONICA

100

<u>Being Spontaneous in The Linear</u>

"In your reality the essence of time is a huge factor in your level of participation. Many adhere to the ticking of the clock closely by planning each and every moment. The culture contributes to this on many levels as well.

The ability to connect with your soul may be distorted by this close adherence to the timeline. One should remember that the soul knows nothing of time. It is only the physical participation that brings it so close to the soulful energy.

It is important to remember that in the linear the choice to be more spontaneous is available. Using your thoughts to create reality need not be defined by the particulars of the hour.

Decide that the feeling of a moment may have the ability to transform your life and your connection with spirit.

Thinking through the moment in its creation is more valuable when coupled with the immediacy of the action.

Do not let the time element distract from the pure essence of the immediate moment. You are indeed able to transform the current energy with great ability.

Being open to change and the energy it brings may be just the thing you need right now.

Eliminate doubt and go with the positive energy of the moment. Pure energy is extremely poignant when enacted without the boundaries of time.

Just be.

Allow.

Be spontaneous.

See what happens."

-VERONICA

"It is all about you discovering yourself. The way the
probabilities will play out for you will be determined by
how much you uncover of the real you
for your eyes to see..."

From: VERONICA

101

Planetary Healing

"The linear moment is upon all of you. It is time to reconnect to your soulful energy. The environment where all participate needs the healing vibration that dwells within you.

Of course there are dramas to evolve but the space that allows participation needs balance as well.

Most of you embark daily upon evolution. Others periodically embrace the opportunity. Wherever you are it is time to blend energetically with the plane that allows you to do so!

Take a moment each day to willfully engage the vibration of the earth. Feel compassion for its sacrifices. Know that by enduring the difficulties it provides a stage to play out your dramas. A better friend no one could have. So therefore with focus, give back so that it may continue the process.

A random universal opportunity awaits those who blend their energy towards the earth. A most giving solid entity, who needs a return of the nurturing.

Put yourself in alignment with the fragrant delivery of its charms. Return the favor with your energy to bring balance and harmony.

This exchange will only empower all who participate. Be the giver. Be the healer. Be you. One with the planet and yourself. Your role is not insignificant!

It's time!"

-VERONICA

102

A Sense of Security in The Linear

"Many levels of energy participate in the linear. There are baby souls, young souls, mature souls, and old souls, etc. All seeking clarity and experience in their physical expressions. The more advanced the energy perhaps the more stable the experience since the older soul would have more criteria to draw upon.

It would seem that the younger souls distracted by all the input would be most at risk of slipping in their secure impressions of their lives.

We would venture to say the linear environments can be volatile for the most experienced of players. The sense of center often elusive to the most advanced of energies. It is easy to become so involved with the linear that one loses the sense of well being within the life.

It is important to separate often from the experience and realign to the core energy that created you unto this existence. There is no security or sense of well being outside the self. It is a random universe with the free will component in place. The "at free will" is the safe guard to the security all would wish for while physical.

Allowing the self to engage in dramas that undermine that sense of well being is the root of all mishap.

One must center themselves within their soul to feel secure. To seek it outside the self will not allow for that sensing to grab hold and maintain the self.

Practice silence internally to find the safe guards all seek while in this place of physical.

Know yourself.

Know your ability to center and then enact it."

-VERONICA

"Physical life from a spiritual perspective is rather like a melody. There are high notes and low notes but it is not the singular note that you will remember... it is the melody... a combination of all the notes that define the vibration of your soul while having the life experience."

From: VERONICA

103

The Next Place of Wonder

"Many participants in their lives are ever seeking the external, the perfect relationship, experience, job, place, etc. As a culture it is taught to seek fulfillment outside the self.

Of course being physical places one in a culture where survival is determined by the amount of physical abundance one has acquired. This is not something we disagree with. It is important to feel safe and secure in your environment. Our concern lies with where one looks to find this abundance.

Much has been said of late about the ability to create what one wants through their thoughts. It is interesting that most move directly towards material things before seeking alignment with their soul.

Having said that, we reiterate the concept of thought creating reality. The way to abundance does not begin externally. It begins in that place of wonder called your soul. If one discovers the beauty and power there, the reality will align its self.

Seek then a relationship with your soulful energy. It will lead you to the next place of wonder.... "abundance," someone once said.

Money does not grow on trees. Abundance, however, grows within you and will manifest according to the energy of your soul and your internal relationship with it.

There is no greater place of wonder."

-VERONICA

104

<u>Listening</u>

"In the linear reality many aspire to be proactive in their participation. They gallantly display their energy to anyone who may be near. Seeking the connection to their existence they often speak of the connection of mind, body, and spirit.

It is a habit of those embodied to speak more than they listen. The resonating tenor of their voice makes them feel productive and vital in the physical environment. It is happening everywhere one looks.... a lot of talkers but very few listeners.

We are sure that the many who have much to say are lacking when it comes to hearing the whispers of their own souls. An unfortunate moment since it is often the subtle expressions that provoke the most growth.

We would advise all who aspire to connect with their souls to listen carefully to the breath of a newborn, the song of a grasshopper, and the cry of a kitten as it searches for its mother.

The vibration of your own soul can be heard on a clear evening in the garden. It is the desire to focus on these simple moments that begins the greatest growth.

Be still.

Listen to the pulse of your soul.

The rhythm will sound out a clear message to your heart. If only you would listen the wonders of the universe would be revealed.

Try.

See what occurs.

Listen."

-VERONICA

~ Notes ~

* * *

About the Author

April Crawford is an AMAZON Top 50 Best Selling Author, but April is also one of the world's most naturally talented and adept Open Deep Trance Channels and Spiritual Mediums.

April Crawford is Internationally known as both an author and as an Open Deep Trance Channel and Spiritual Medium, with clients in most countries of the world.

About The Author

April's spiritual newsletter, *"Inner Whispers"*, is written by highly evolved nonphysical entities and guides and is read by tens of thousands of readers each week. It is available (free) at www.InnerWhispers.net

April currently lives in Los Angeles, California with her husband, Allen, and her many pets

***

Other Books by April Crawford

OTHER BOOKS
BY
APRIL CRAWFORD

"Inner Whispers": Messages From A Spirit Guide (Volume I)

Available also as Kindle Book

For more information:

www.InnerWhispersTheBook.com

"Parting Notes": A Connection With The Afterlife

Also available as an E-Book at

www.AprilCrawfordBookstore.com

Also available as a Kindle Book

For more information: www.PartingNotes.com

Other Books by April Crawford

Ashram Tang... a Story... and a Discovery
Also available a Kindle Book.
www.AshramTang.com

Reflections of a Spiritual Astronaut: Book I

Available as an E-Book at
www.AprilCrawfordBookstore.com
Also available as a Kindle Book.

Reflections of a Spiritual Astronaut: Book II

Available as an E-Book at
www.AprilCrawfordBookstore.com
Also available as a Kindle Book.

your life and its choices: THE RECIPE FOR ASCENTION TO ANOTHER PLANE "A" TO "Z"
By Ish and Osco (Spirit Guides) via April Crawford

Available as a Kindle Book.

Other Books by April Crawford

For more information about the Author or about True
Open Deep Trance Channeling:
www.AprilCrawford.com

For the free spiritual newsletter *"Inner Whispers"*
www.InnerWhispers.net

For personal telephone or in-person consultations via
April Crawford, Personal Appearances, or Media
Interviews contact Allen at AprilReadings@aol.com

***

Made in the USA
San Bernardino, CA
02 January 2013